Music Minus One Vocals

Songs In The Style Of

KRISTIN
Chenoweth

2166

Music Minus One
50 Executive Boulevard • Elmsford, New York 10523-1325
914-592-1188 • e-mail: info@musicminusone.com
www.musicminusone.com

Songs In The Style Of

KRISTIN Chenoweth

CONTENTS

ISBN 978-1-941566-66-4

MMO 2166

If You Hadn't But You Did

Jule Styne
Betty Comden and Adolph Green

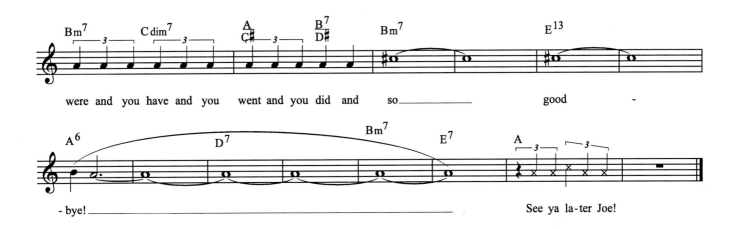

were and you have and you went and you did and so_____ good -

- bye!_____ See ya la-ter Joe!

How Long Has This Been Going On?

George Gershwin and Ira Gershwin

'Neath the stars at ba-zaars of-ten I've had to car - ress men,

five or ten dol-lars then I'd col-lect from all those "yes" men. Don't be sad, I must add that they meant no more than

chess men._ Dar-ling can't you see 'twas for char-i-ty. Though these lips have made slips, it was ne-ver real-ly ser-i-ous.

Who'd have thought I'd be brought to a state that's so de - li-ri-ous? I could cry sal-ty tears,

where have I been all these years?_ Lit-tle wow, tell me now, how

My Funny Valentine

Richard Rodgers and Lorenz Hart

10

MMO 2166

Hangin' Around With You

George Gershwin and Ira Gershwin

The Girl In 14G

Richard Scanlon, Jeanine Tesori

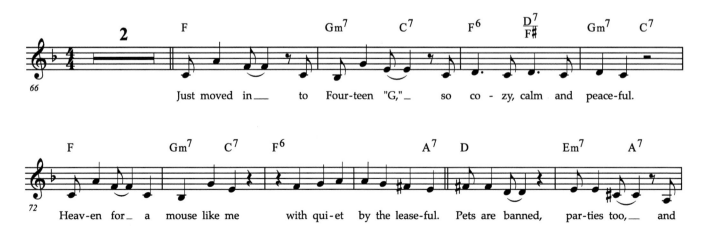

G Em7 Am7 D7 G G#dim7 Am7 D7 G Em7

Thir - teen, Fif - teen, Four-teen "G."_ A most un - like - ly tri - o. Not quite three-part

Am7 D7 **Faster** G Cm6

har - mo - ny.__ All day all night we're sing-in. "Zoot doo doot floy doy_ a zee bop boo doo

boy ta boy." "Stop!"_____ "Ah._____

A♭7 / C D7 **Slower swing** G Em7

_____ Ah."_____ Had my fill of

Am7 D7 G F#7 G7 G#7 A7 G#7 A7 B♭7 Am9

peace and qui - et. Shout out loud._ I've changed my di - et, all be-cause_ of

D7 G

Four - teen "G!"_____

I'll Tell The Man On The Street

Richard Rodgers and Lorenz Hart

Rit. **Freely** Cmaj7 Dm7 G7 Cmaj7 Em7 Dm7 G7

4   2

I won't tell of my love to the red, red rose_____ or the

I'm A Stranger Here Myself

Ogden Nash and Kurt Weill

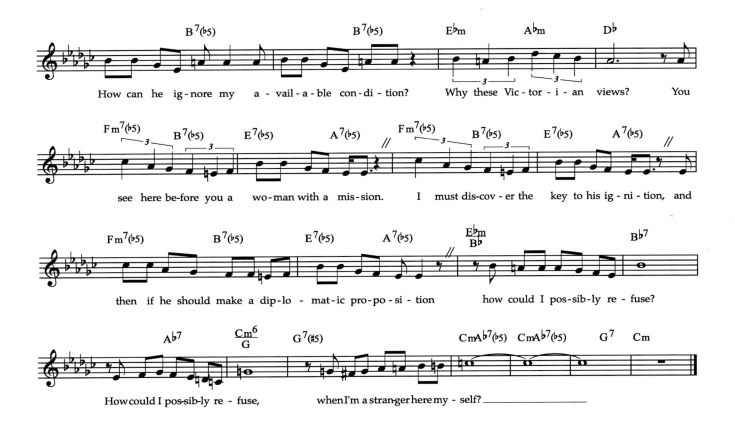

Nobody Else But Me

Oscar Hammerstein II and Jerome Kern

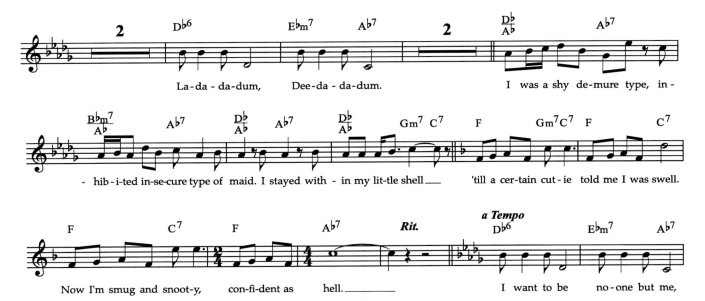

I am in love with a lov-er who likes me the way I am.___ I have my faults,

he likes my fault;___ I'm not ve-ry bright, he's not ve-ry bright. He thinks I'm grand,

that's grand for me. We may be wrong but if we get a-long why do we care, say we. When he holds me close,
I get a thrill know-ing he gets a thrill when I sit on his knee. Walk-ing on the shore,

close as we can be I tell the lad that I'm grate-ful and I'm glad that I'm
swim-ming in the sea. When I am with him, I'm glad that girl who's with him is

no-bod-y else but me. me. When he holds me close, close as we can be,
no-bod-y else but___

I tell the lad that I'm grate-ful and I'm glad that I'm no-bod-y else but me.___

Nobody's Heart Belongs To Me / Why Can't I?

Richard Rodgers and Lorenz Hart

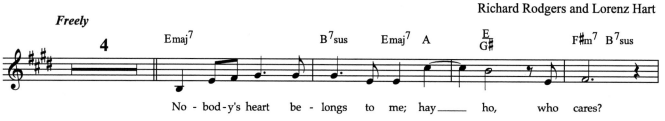

No-bod-y's heart be-longs to me; hay___ ho, who cares?

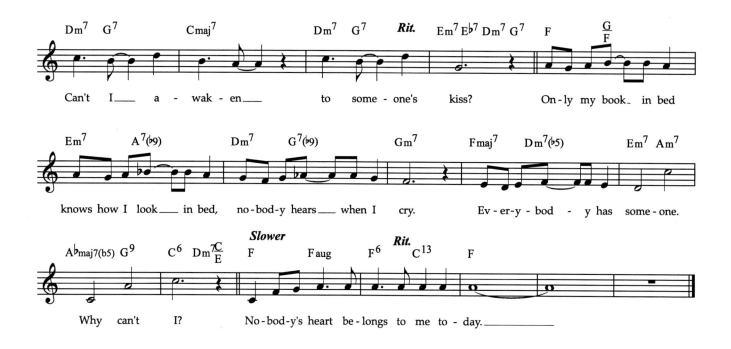

Can't I a-wak-en to some-one's kiss? On-ly my book in bed knows how I look in bed, no-bod-y hears when I cry. Ev-er-y-bod-y has some-one. Why can't I? No-bod-y's heart be-longs to me to-day.

Going To The Dance With You

Richard A. Dworsky

The rain my fall, the wind may blow, It may get down to twen-ty be-low. I don't mind, 'cause I'm go-ing to the dance with you. The rent's un-paid, the cup-board's bare, I won't cry, I won't de-spair, no. I don't mind, 'cause I'm go-ing to the dance with you. And when the or-ches-tra plays so sweet and low, I'll

I'm in love and I'm go-ing to the dance with you.

You'll Never Know

Mack Gordon and Henry Warren

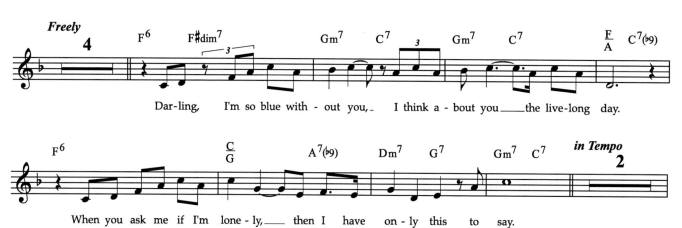

Dar-ling, I'm so blue with-out you, I think a-bout you the live-long day.

When you ask me if I'm lone-ly, then I have on-ly this to say.

You'll ne-ver know just how much I miss you, you'll ne-ver know just how

much I care. And if I tried, I still could-n't hide my

love for you. You ought to know, for have-n't I told you so a

mil-lion or more times? You went a-way and my heart went with you,

I____ speak your name_ in my ev - 'ry prayer. If there is some____ oth-er way to prove____ that I love you, I swear I don't know how. You'll____ ne-ver know_ if you don't know now.____ You____ went a - way____ and my heart went with you,____ I____ speak your name_ in my ev - 'ry prayer. If there is some___ oth-er way to prove____ that I love you, I swear I don't know how. You'll____ ne-ver know____ if you don't know now.____

Taylor The Latte Boy

Zina Goodrich and Marcy Heisler

There's a boy who works at Star - buck's who is ve - ry ins - pir-a-tion-al, he is

26

MMO 2166

Music Minus One
50 Executive Boulevard • Elmsford, New York 10523-1325   914-592-1188 • e-mail: info@musicminusone.com
www.musicminusone.com

MMO 2166
ISBN 978-1-941566-66-4